JEWELLERY

LEARNING
RESOURCES
CENTRE

MAKE YOUR OWN

JEWELLERY

Christa Nölling · Kyra Stempell

Bath · New York · Singapore · Hong Kong · Cologne · Delhi · Melbourne

This edition published in 2010
Copyright © 2007 Parragon Books Ltd
Queen Street House
4 Queen Street
Bath BA1 1 HE, UK

Original edition produced by: ditter.projektagentur GmbH
Project coordination: Michael Ditter
Photography: Ruprecht Stempell
Models: Katja Janzon, Svenja Nölling-Petry, Jenny Cremer
Layout: Christa Nölling

We would like to thank the following people for their support:
Bettina Flügel, 'Bettinas Bastelstübchen', 50181 Bedburg (materials procurement)
Heike Döring, Bedburg-Kaster (advice on 'Felting')
Gisela Schanzenberger (advice and support on 'Nature Jewellery' and 'Beading')

English edition produced by: Cambridge Publishing Management Ltd
Translator: Tess Pike
Copy-editor: Sandra Stafford
Proofreader: Juliet Mozley
Project editor: Alison Coupe

ISBN: 978-1-4454-0563-6
Printed in Indonesia

Contents

PART 1

Making your own jewellery...

... a hobby for you

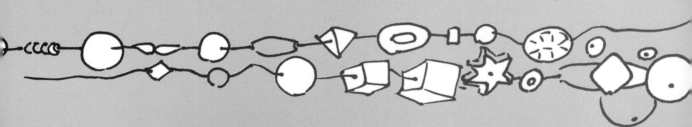

What is the fascination of jewellery?

Our wish to adorn ourselves is as old as nature itself. And it isn't just people who take pleasure in decorating themselves. Far from it: our role models lie in the colourful blossoms of the flowers that attract bees, in animal calls and in the shimmering plumage of birds. So it's not at all surprising that we became attracted to the idea of jewellery for ourselves, too.

The history of jewellery

Jewellery has always been an important symbol of power, rank and religion. The craft and artisan skills of a period are reflected by the jewellery of the time. Indeed, by looking at who adorned themselves with what, we can gain a valuable insight into the values and level of knowledge of a particular culture.

Originally jewellery took the form of an amulet, which was reputed to avert danger and bring good luck. This was the start of jewellery's progression towards its role as a means to create an aesthetic impression, a personal display. We owe much of what we know today about the history of jewellery to the tradition of grave jewellery. It was believed that the dead should not pass on to 'the other side' without means, so rich gifts – including jewellery – were laid in the grave.

Another important source is representations on statues, reliefs and pictures that show us the jewellery traditions of different cultures.

Similarities in styles of jewellery allow us to identify which peoples traded with each other. This early form of international exchange generated new designs and inspiration. Raw materials were exchanged as well as ideas and craftsmanship.

Even finds from the Stone Age, which are 75,000 years old, reveal pierced and coloured snail shells which were probably worn as beads on a chain.

The enhanced possibilities provided by metal and glass working that began in the Bronze Age and continued to develop over the following periods produced increasingly varied shapes and kinds of jewellery. The piercing of gemstone beads was discovered in Egypt 3,500 years before our time. But even then, during the early days of jewellery making, ways were being sought to overcome shortages of raw materials and develop new ones. Fashion jewellery had begun its triumphal march.

Fashion jewellery: no phenomenon of our time

It is fascinating to note that the history of jewellery and the development of fashion jewellery correspond to the history and economic and moral backgrounds of an era. Times of prosperity and peace were almost always accompanied by artistic diversity, by a wish to adorn oneself and by advances in craftsmanship. Such times of plenty were also reflected at a social level, with the education of a broad band of the middle classes. Jewellery was not just the preserve of the aristocracy, but was worn by a wide cross-section of the population in a variety of forms.

The **Phoenicians** and **Etruscans** had already been adept at producing fine jewellery using semi-precious materials. They developed a form of gold leaf in order to create a valuable surface appearance,

and they were masters at copying precious stones. Each culture developed its own main emphasis: while the Greeks perceived the material value as being more important than the aesthetic design, the Etruscans favoured lavish naturalistic displays.

In the era of **Hellenism**, jewellery experienced a true golden age. A large middle class in Ancient Greece demanded a wide variety of motifs and forms of jewellery. Necklaces, earrings, tiaras and diadems, hairnet caps, brooches, arm bangles and rings were much sought after. The materials used were gold, various metals, pearls, garnets, emeralds and amethysts.

For the **Romans**, however, jewellery was purely and simply a status symbol. Despite this, a few affluent people chose to wear ornamental rings made from copper, iron or bronze with an inset of glass. It is this era that spawned the 'melon beads', painted pebble ceramics that looked surprisingly like real pearls.

With the demise of the Western Roman Empire came the end of the first great period of fashion jewellery. The next impetus came from **Byzantium**, later Constantinople and present-day Istanbul, to where many scholars and artists of the Western world had retreated. Enamelling, the technique of 'Opus Interasile' – a filigree cut work technique – and mosaic works (tessellation) were refined. Christian motifs were already evident on many pieces of jewellery.

'Nature creates nothing
without a purpose.'

Aristotle

of antiquity, which began in the 14th century as a spiritual movement and gained ground in the following centuries, particularly in the area of art. This age was characterized by a desire to create a new style based on antiquity. Greek scholars, who had moved to Venice and other Italian towns following the conquest of Constantinople by the Turks in 1453, brought the knowledge of the culture of Greek antiquity with them.

For the first time, jewellery and clothing developed in parallel and influenced each other mutually. In the late 14th century a process for cutting diamonds was invented, leading to their increased use in jewellery design.

This was also a time when jewellery manufacturers were still heavily dependent on their aristocratic clients, but the desire for opulent jewellery was spreading within society. Venice was one of the leading jewellery centres of the period. Pearls and precious stones were traded there, but it was the art of glass making and pearl imitations that was of the greatest importance. Gilded metals and stones backed with foil gave the jewellery industry a tremendous boost. Even today the island of Murano is world-famous for its glassware.

In **Europe** there then followed a period during which jewellery had no great significance. The German migrations (375–568) meant that the continent was rarely at peace, and during the Middle Ages that followed, for a period of almost 1,000 years, jewellery was regarded merely as a method of payment, not as ornamentation. Furthermore, the dominance of the aristocracy and strict legal statutes regarding the manufacture of jewellery prevented the artistic and technical advancement of this decorative art.

Renaissance of jewellery

Jewellery design experienced a renewed period of prosperity with the **Renaissance**, the cultural rebirth

Freedom in the Baroque

Following long periods of war in the first half of the 17th century, the economic and political situation in Europe continued to stabilize. The desire grew for affordable jewellery and luxury. The **Baroque** period began. Fashion allowed more of the arms to be exposed, so there was more space for jewellery. Trade ties were expanded; precious stones were imported and assumed mystic significance. This period also saw the birth of the first short fashion movements. These developments were boosted by two ground-breaking discoveries. In France a process for imitating pearls was developed whereby weighted glass beads were painted with a solution made from fish scales, then coated with wax. And in 1675, English chemist **George Ravenscroft** invented glass paste, a lead glass with similar properties to precious stones that could be easily cut. This signified the birth of lead crystal. The triumphal march of fashion jewellery could no longer be halted.

Strass and Pinchbeck

The **Industrial Revolution** began in England in the 18th century, and in the 19th century spread from there to Europe and America. Englishman James Watt invented the steam engine, which facilitated new methods of production and the building of the first factories. The strict class system between the aristocracy and the bourgeoisie was largely lifted and an affluent middle class emerged. These developments boosted the potential for the production of fashion jewellery and generated very high demand. It was this period which, for the first time, saw differentiation being made between daytime and evening jewellery. The first women's magazines – still coloured by hand – showed changing fashion movements and awakened new desires.

At the same time **Georges Frédéric Strass** invented his namesake, the 'Strass Diamond' – the rhinestone – which even nowadays has the power to influence fashion. Strass's jewellery designs were popular not only among the affluent middle classes, but also

within the highest circles of the aristocracy. In 1734 he was appointed to the post of 'Jeweller to the King of France'. This elevated even fashion jewellery to the realms of the aristocratic classes. Strass went as far as to copy modern pieces made from precious stones and exhibit his imitations alongside the real works in his shop. This elevated the perfection and brilliance of the imitations yet further because amateurs could hardly tell the difference between these and the originals.

At the same time, London watchmaker **Christopher Pinchbeck** was developing a copper and zinc alloy, which is now named after him – pinchbeck. The result looked like gold, was better to work with, was extremely cheap and could be manufactured in series production from castings. From now on, it was used predominantly for the production of shoe buckles and watch casings, and was frequently combined with rhinestones. You can still find 'pinchbeck jewellery' these days.

Quick fashion change

There followed a long period of unrest and wars in Europe and America, which left little scope for luxury. Various regional undercurrents developed, which reflected the mood and political and economic situation in individual countries. Purchasing power was reduced, with the result that real jewellery once again became limited to just the aristocracy and the upper classes. Meanwhile industrialization had significantly progressed, and the techniques developed by Strass and Pinchbeck continued to be perfected. Steel jewellery, which was by now much sought after, began to be predominantly machine finished from 1830, and also in the 19th century, plastic, rubber and aluminium extended the spectrum of artificial materials. Jewellery was designed on a more individual basis, and the differences between individual fashion movements were already becoming markedly shortened.

Art nouveau: the dawn of a new age

With the end of the 19th century, calls for a new form of art were becoming louder. The time was right for increasing individuality and turning away from strict shapes and guidelines. It was the time of 'art nouveau'.

From 1895, Parisian jewellery designer **René Lalique** pioneered a new approach to jewellery, drawing his inspiration from the shapes of nature: plants, blossoms, insects and fish. His preferred materials were glass, enamel, mother-of-pearl, ivory and horn. He placed the artistic merits of an object significantly above its intrinsic value – a concept that proved extremely successful. Other famous jewellers of this period were **Georges Fouquet**

(who designed exclusive pieces of jewellery for the actress Sarah Bernhardt), **Lucien Gaillard** (who was particularly inspired by Japanese art) and **La Maison Vever** (the company founded by brothers **Paul** and **Henri Vever**).

A designer's name became the trademark, and the cult surrounding great actresses and chorus girls heralded a new golden age of fashion jewellery. Strass jewellery became popular again and **Daniel Swarovski** took the fashion world by storm with his high-quality cut stones from the Tyrol.

Art deco: a revival

In 1925, an 'Exposition Internationale des Arts Décoratifs' was held in Paris, and it was the title of this exhibition that inspired the term 'art deco'. The art deco period was characterized by elegant, clear lines, cool, strong colours and prosaic practicality, which nonetheless emanated sensual appeal. The women of the time were emancipated and self-confident – an outlook they were keen to reflect in their fashions. This resulted in the emphasis of 1920s and 1930s jewellery design being on cool aesthetics and extravagance. Besides precious metals, jewellery was also made from chrome, jade, ebony, jet (which is still attributed with magical powers) and plastics. The artists chose as their motifs mainly abstract fruit, leaves or blossoms, as well as geometric shapes and Cubist elements.

'I freed women's bodies.' **Gabriella 'Coco' Chanel** appeared to the public as self-assured as her customers themselves were. Emancipated, independent, with strings of imitation pearl necklaces, costume jewellery and short hair, she became a model for many women. This trend was encouraged by cheap cultured pearls, which were supplied from Japan all over the world from 1920. Combs, brooches, earrings and stick pins completed the overall look. For a while it also became fashionable to wear black and white, hence the trend for combining the whiteness of diamonds or rock crystal with black onyx or enamel.

The French fashion designer **Christian Dior** was also deemed an enthusiastic advocate of fashion jewellery, considering it an entity in its own right completely detached from the appearance of real jewellery. Fantasy and exuberance were key elements, and the 'Maison Schiaparelli' founded in 1928 by Italian **Elsa Schiaparelli** stood out for being particularly imaginative. Using wood, porcelain, glass and amber, Elsa transformed clothing fasteners, buttons and hooks into striking pieces of jewellery.

In Germany, the 'Weimar Bauhaus' (1919) defined jewellery design. Spheres, cones, cuboids and rhombuses characterized the shapes and designs. In **North America** the fashion jewellery market was also very active, even during the Great Depression of the 1930s and 1940s. Brightness and gaiety were the order of the day, and semi-precious stones were combined with colourful metals. During the Second World War jewellery production moved almost exclusively to America. Because of the general shortage of raw materials, those most commonly used were silver, cast metal, horn, bone and wood. **Dior** created his first fashion jewellery collection. **Trifari** designed flowers with invisible settings. But jewellery increasingly lost its aesthetic value, becoming once again an object of material worth.

Changing fashions

With the 1950s and a renewed upturn in the national mood, the desire for beauty and jewellery also experienced a boom. The centre of world trade remained in America. Diamonds were high fashion among the rich upper classes; fashion jewellery was popular everywhere. Famous fashion houses of the time – **Dior**, **Trifari**, **Tiffany** and **Chanel** – produced creative designs that reflected the spirit of the age. The 1960s were characterized by gold, which was combined with precious or semi-precious stones to create striking pieces of jewellery.

The **trend towards individualization** gained increasing speed. Societies were characterized by groups that wanted to express their ideologies in their fashion. Hippies, punks, the disco wave – they all had their own philosophy on life and the world, which they expressed with striking and individual pieces of jewellery. Real jewellery was perceived as being timeless and for eternity. Fashion jewellery was for showing one's own mood to the world. Inspiration was frequently drawn from jewellery of the past. The hippies took Indian jewellery as their model, the glitter of Strass and metal typified the disco era, and businesswomen wore brooches in the art deco style. The punk uniform relied on rivets, leather and metal.

The trend of the future will be towards an ever-increasing individuality. We will be free to develop our own style. Anyone who likes gold can pass on silver. If you like large, eye-catching jewellery, you don't need to wait for it to come back into fashion. Each one of us can be a trendsetter.

The materials...

Glass beads

Pearls are a sensual pleasure, pure and unadulterated. They allow us to dream; they catch and reflect light. Pearls are always different. They glimmer gently, sparkle majestically or shrink back into themselves.

Pearls reflect our souls. This is one of their secrets. The other is their evolution. Even today we still don't know exactly how and why real 'freshwater' pearls grow in their shells. It is said that when an oyster is injured, a grain of sand slips in and sometimes develops into a beautiful pearl. Pearls keep their mystery and give us their beauty.

Glass beads may not be as valuable, but they are no less fascinating. There are no barriers to the imagination either in the shape, colour or combination. There are seed beads, wax pearls, Swarovski® crystals, rosette beads, lozenge beads and many more.

When combining beads, it is important to pay close attention to colour coordination. Often, less is more! You should aim to wear your glass bead jewellery with clothing in muted colours. This shows the jewellery to best advantage and is also most flattering to you.

Nature

Nature jewellery is an expression of primitiveness. Nature and its living organisms are constantly decorating themselves – to impress members of the same species or else to protect themselves. We find it fascinating to change our own appearance.

Nature provides a range of ideas and the materials to match – such as wood, feathers, shells, stones, leather and metal. Each of these is already remarkable in itself, but they can also be combined to make completely new, wonderful creations.

Because the materials are so unique, you can always find new inspiration for personal items of jewellery by watching and investigating the environment. You will be surprised what you can discover during a walk through the wood or along the beach!

Felt

Felt jewellery is very individual and unique. The intensive manipulation of the wool creates small marvels that always develop a pattern of their own. Every felted work of art generally conforms to the designer's plan, but still has individual idiosyncrasies and peculiarities.

The special thing about felting is the complex technique used to process the wool. In this book we explain the technique of wet felting using soapsuds. During the felting process, the wool becomes increasingly stronger, but also offers scope for changing the shape, colour or pattern. Felt can be combined to very good effect with beads and metal components, giving it a completely different character.

During felting you will see and feel how the material changes, and you will discover more and more new ideas for shapes and combinations. Felt is fascinating!

Colour Melt Crystals

The pleasure of working with Colour Melt Crystals lies in their dramatic transformation. These tiny crystals turn into solid blocks, the shapes and colours of which are entirely up to the individual. Nothing has already been decided. You can do anything with these crystals – it's completely up to you.

Even after melting, the resulting block can be manipulated and shaped while still warm. Melting and hardening can also be done in several stages, so that the piece of jewellery can continue to be changed and perfected.

Colour Melt Crystals are an artificial product and not particularly valuable. But the results can be very personal. You could, for example, make small charms for necklaces or belts, and embed keepsakes within them.

They are also ideal for making highly personal presents and gifts for one's nearest and dearest.

'You only have to do something with lots of love for it to be met with luck.'

Johannes Trojan

PART 2

Making your own jewellery...

... how to do it!

Every material needs its own tools and has its own techniques. But there are a few general things that you need to remember to make sure your jewellery turns out right and looks good.

A few general tips...

1. Read the instructions in this chapter carefully. If you're not sure about what you're doing while you're working on a piece of jewellery, just turn back to these tips.

2. Take your time! You can't just fit making your jewellery into small slots of time; you need to give the materials your full attention, otherwise you won't get any pleasure from it.

3. Ensure that you work with clean and dry hands on a clean, protected surface.

4. The boxes at the top of the page for each set of instructions show the difficulty rating of the piece of jewellery (see for example page 34). One filled-in box indicates that the piece is easy to make; two boxes means average difficulty; and three boxes are real masterpieces. Try them out, but first familiarize yourself with the techniques required.

5. We have specified colours and shapes. If you prefer other colours, allow your creativity free rein. But try to make sure the colours harmonize well together. The pieces of jewellery should not be too colourful. This applies particularly to the beads, because they are so striking. Often, less is more!

Glass beads…

… are readily available in a seemingly endless variety. Therefore, this book uses lots of different kinds of beads of varying colours and shapes. At the same time we are keen to give you a free hand if you want to try another variation. This book provides useful tips and valuable ideas, but we would encourage you to develop your own ideas, too.

Just a few important things for you to consider…

The large, colourful, shiny beads are, of course, the focal point of every piece of jewellery, but can be changed.

Which beads you use is a matter of personal taste. However, there are also small, almost invisible beads – known as **seed beads** or simply **glass beads** – which have a very important function: they act as spacers, enhancing the appearance of a piece of jewellery, and they add strength. If these beads are mentioned, it is important that you use them!

There are lots of kinds of jewellery fasteners, and sometimes you don't even need to put in a separate fastener at all.

Sometimes the ends of a piece of jewellery can be linked by means of two loops made using **crimp beads**. These are even more inconspicuous than seed beads, but are incredibly useful: you thread them on to the jewellery wire, one before and one after the bead you wish to fix, press them together using bent nose pliers, and your bead is fixed into position.

Alternatively, you thread a crimp bead at least $^{1}/_{2}$in (1cm) from the end of the thread or wire, bend over the end of the wire, lead it back through the crimp bead and press it together. You have one loop. If you loop a second loop around the first one before you close it, you have a simple but very effective fastener.

Jump rings can also be attached to these loops as a link between the wire and any kind of fastener. The important thing to remember is that you mustn't pull the ring outwards when you open it, but – using round nose pliers and bent nose pliers – pull one part towards you and push the other away. This prevents the ring from getting deformed, and helps it to keep its strength.

Jewellery wire is used a lot in this book. Try winding the wire on to a thick bobbin before you start crafting. This will ensure it remains smooth and can be properly unrolled. Once jewellery wire gets kinked, it cannot be smoothed out again.

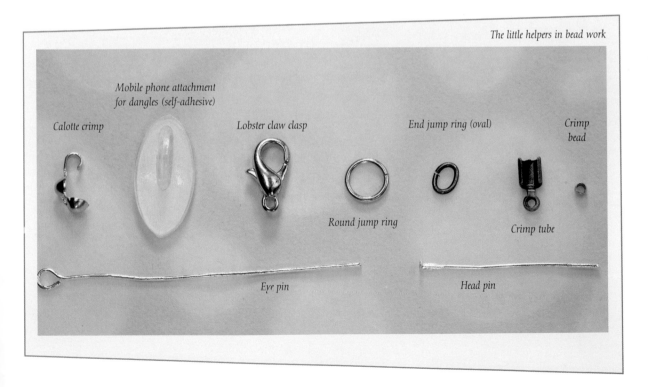

The little helpers in bead work

Calotte crimp

Mobile phone attachment for dangles (self-adhesive)

Lobster claw clasp

End jump ring (oval)

Crimp bead

Round jump ring

Crimp tube

Eye pin

Head pin

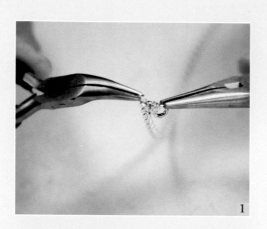

Tools

1. This picture shows a strong double-act: bent nose pliers (left) and round nose pliers. You use one pair to hold the piece of jewellery while the other shapes the ring or bends the wire. You will need to use these two tools over and over again – particularly for beadwork.

2. The last member of the pliers team is a pair of side-cutting pliers. You can use these to cut through cable chains and wires cleanly and easily.

3. This picture shows the round nose pliers and bent nose pliers in action. We use the bent nose pliers to thread the head pin through the link, while the round nose pliers shape the end of the head pin into a round ring, thus securing the piece of jewellery to the cable chain.

'The setting of precious stones increases their price, not their value.'

Ludwig Börne

Techniques

4. For fixing: thread crimp beads on to the wire, one before and one after the bead you wish to fix. Use the round nose pliers to press the crimp beads together. This allows beads to be fixed, but to appear to be 'floating freely' on a thread or a thin wire. If you want to make a loop, take the end of the thread, pass it in a loop back through the crimp bead, then press it together.

5. This picture shows an open jump ring. To do this, hold the ring with the round nose pliers and bent nose pliers, then gently bend one side towards you and the other away from you. This prevents the basic shape of the ring from being distorted and means it retains its strength.

6. This is the end of a head pin. Leave a little less than 1/2in. (1 cm) protruding and use the round nose pliers to bend the end into a loop. Make sure the loop is firmly closed. You can thread this loop directly through another finding (a cable chain, eyelet or fastener). Alternatively, you can attach a jump ring on to it, which you then hook into a cable chain or fastener.

Nature jewellery

The materials used here come from nature: metal, leather, feathers, mother-of-pearl, bast fibre and wool. You can also incorporate shells, wood or other natural materials in your own designs. Because of the gentle colour tones, the materials harmonize incredibly well. The most effective thing to do is use similar shades of colour and different shapes. This shows the jewellery to particularly good advantage.

The crafting techniques are very varied. There are no set techniques; you are free to do whatever appeals.

An important focus of this section of the book is working with **rivets** and **eyelets**. There are various techniques, depending on the tools used.

First you have to punch the holes, for which you'll need a pair of **punch pliers**. You will also need a piece of thick leather to place between your piece of work and the lower part of the punch pliers. Now punch the hole. The leather doesn't only make it easier, it also allows you to protect the cutting edge of the punch pliers, which would otherwise get blunt very quickly.

You can buy rivets and eyelets from stockists of craft and jewellery supplies. In each packet there is a simple tool with instructions. If you use the tool provided, you will also need a hammer to drive the rivets into the holes. Work on a firm, unbreakable and protected surface – preferably a workbench.

It is easier to use a **hand riveter**. You place the rivets into the indents in the riveter, then press them into the ready-made holes. If you prefer, you could check whether a shoe-mender's or key-cutter's or a shop that sells sewing goods could do this for you.

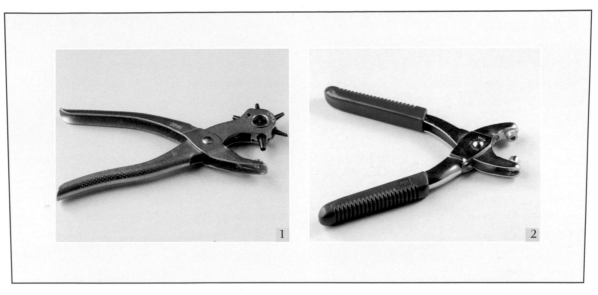

1. You use the punch pliers to punch the holes for the rivets. Place a thick piece of leather on the punching plate of the punch pliers, then lay the workpiece on top of it. This makes it easier, and the cutting edge of the punch pliers won't get blunt so quickly.

2. The hand riveter is not included in the packet with the rivets. The riveter is easier to use than the plastic plate supplied and a hammer, but the principle is the same.

Tools and techniques

3. The pictures show you how to do it. You take the two parts of the rivet and the riveter. Then you place the upper part of the rivet in the hole…

4. … and place the lower part on the rivet plate. Finally, position the piece of leather and press the riveter together over the hole. The rivet is now fixed.

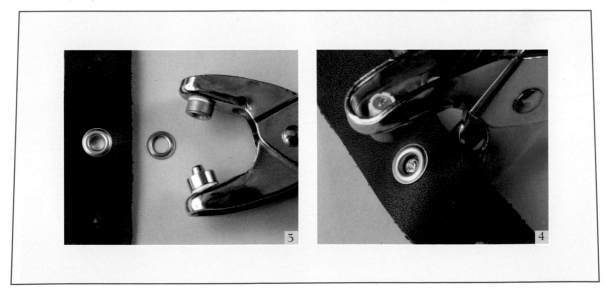

Felting

Working with felting wool – sometimes also called 'magic wool' – requires a certain amount of patience and skill, but is tremendous fun. Using simple materials you can create wonderful patterns and shapes. The material offers lots of surprises because during the felting process the wool substantially changes its consistency and size.

You only need a few tools and materials to felt. Use a **rubber mat** to work on. Car mats are ideal for this, as their structure also gives the material rigidity.

You can use a **spray bottle** or **laundry sprinkler** to dampen the material carefully and evenly.

Gauze or **fly screen mesh** prevents the wool fibres from sticking to your hands during the soaping process.

The only thing you need now is a **bowl of warm water** and a little **curd or olive oil soap**, and of course the **magic wool**.

Magic wool is so called because it feels very soft and silky, and the yarns are available in wonderful colours.

Tools

The picture above shows everything – apart from the felting wool – that you need for felting.

1. A laundry sprinkler. If you can't find one, use a spray bottle. But be careful not to wet the wool too much.

2. A rubber mat. Because of its structure, a car mat is perfect for working the wool. A smooth rubber mat is not ideal, but is still perfectly adequate if it's all you have.

3. Gauze or fly screen mesh.

4. You need bubble wrap to make the jewellery bag.

5. A medium-sized bowl with warm water. Lay the piece of curd or olive oil soap in it, and you will get amazing suds.

What do you need to be aware of?

1. Felted projects are always made from a single piece of felt! Sewing individual pieces together is a no-no among 'felt experts'!

2. The area you start off with must be approximately twice as large as the size you want to achieve in the end. The felting process makes the material shrink.

3. The magic wool should be plucked out, not cut. The best thing to do is to pull individual fibres out using the balls of the thumbs. This is easier and more even than using the fingertips.

4. Only ever use warm water. If the water gets cold, change it as you work.

5. Two felted parts cannot be joined together once they've been made. The only fibres that will link together are two dry or one dry and one wet fibre.

6. Make sure you don't use too much soap.

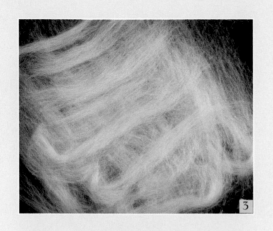

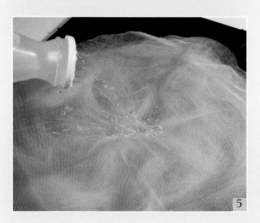

How do you make felt?

The basic steps in felt making are always similar.

1. Using the balls of the thumbs, carefully pull thin fibres from the magic wool. Lay these in the desired shape on your rubber mat.

2. Make sure you lay the fibres out straight and that no loops form. These would get knotted.

3. Then lay another thin layer on top at a right angle. You should still just be able to see the mat through the wool – don't make the wool layers too thick.

4. Cut the gauze to the appropriate shape and lay it on top.

5. Carefully moisten the gauze with warm water from the laundry sprinkler.

6. The first step in the felting process is to gently brush the wool with soap and water through the gauze.

7. During this process turn the pieces round several times, making sure the gauze is always on the top.

8. Once the wool begins to firm up, use your hands to brush more vigorously across the top of the gauze.

9. Now rinse everything under hot water. The water should be as hot as possible, so you may need to wear rubber gloves.

10. Now it's time to full (fluff up) the felt. Knead and roll the felt pieces backwards and forwards on the rubber mat until they get smaller and firmer. At the same time, pinch out the felted wool to achieve the desired shape.

11. Once you've finished felting, allow the pieces to dry naturally. To speed the drying process try rolling larger pieces between hand towels.

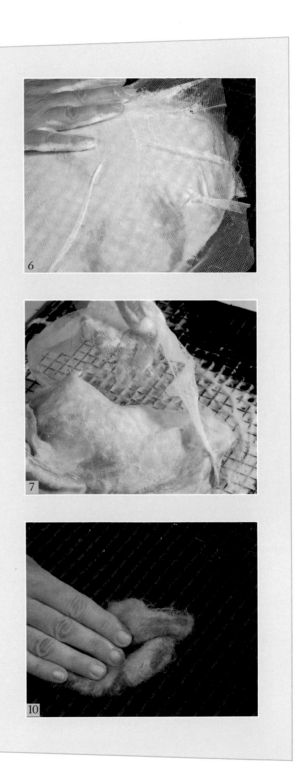

Colour Melt Crystals

What you should know...

Colour Melt Crystals (see page 91) are melted in the oven on a baking tray covered with tinfoil or baking parchment. Set the oven to top and bottom heat, not on air-circulation! The temperature should be set to a maximum of 350°F (180°C). You can also use a lower temperature. This lengthens the melting time, but the resulting smell is less intense. Every time you use Colour Melt Crystals you must clean the oven and ventilate the kitchen afterwards!

Depending on the surface structure wanted – grainy or smooth – melting takes between 20 and 30 minutes. The longer the time, the smoother the effect! Don't be surprised that, when it's cooling, the material shrinks and makes clicking and cracking sounds. This is completely normal. Once it's completely cooled, the disc can be easily removed from the mould.

During the melting process a sharp edge – a burr – usually forms or there may be some surface imperfections. Use a file to smooth them out.

You get a matt finish by roughening up the smooth surface with the dry, abrasive side of a washing-up pad.

To make a hole for hanging the disc after the melted crystals have cooled, use a hot knitting needle or drill a hole using a fine drill head. Alternatively, before melting you can make little rolls out of tinfoil or aluminium strip and position them in the mould in the desired position. The foil then goes into the oven with the melt crystals and is removed after cooling. Choose your preferred method and stick to it, regardless of what it says in the particular instructions that you are following.

The findings used in the book (see page 23) are made from silver-plated brass. If you prefer to use nickel-free findings, it is advisable to source them from a craft shop and check that they are nickel-free.

You need these tools when working with Colour Melt Crystals. A drill with the smallest drill head for boring holes in the cooled disc, or – alternatively – aluminium strip or tinfoil, that you shape into rolls and position in the mould before putting in the oven to keep the holes clear. A file to smooth the raised edges – the burr – on the edge. The dry, abrasive side of a washing-up pad, to give the smooth surface a matt finish. Moulds in different sizes available from craft shops or, alternatively, use pastry cutters.

Working with Colour Melt Crystals
(see page 91) is easy and uncomplicated.
The individual steps are repeated with
every piece of jewellery or accessory.
What makes this technique so special is
the versatility and variety: you can mix
colours, make patterns (see photo left:
mould with heart shape) or embed other
items.

This is how to make the crystal discs.

1. Fill the mould to halfway with crystals,
   pre-heat the oven, then melt the
   crystals. Always check the instructions
   on the packet.

2. Remove the melted crystals (and
   mould) from the oven and leave to
   cool. If you want to change the shape,
   you have to do this while the solidified
   crystals are still warm. But make sure
   the mould isn't still too hot.

3. Once completely cooled the solid disc
   can easily be removed from the mould.
   Now you can drill any holes.

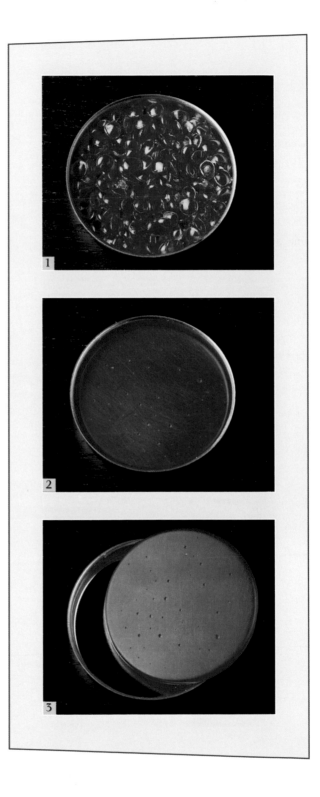

PART 3

Great jewellery…

… for cool girls!

This section shows you various articles of jewellery and fashion accessories made from a variety of materials. Once you've had a little more practice, you'll be able to make up some new ideas of your own, too.

Unleash your creativity. As you work, you'll see how every piece of jewellery develops a character of its own. Even if you stick closely to our instructions, your jewellery will still look a little different from our examples once it's finished. That's the wonderful thing about it.

Take your time, work carefully, and enjoy the distinctiveness and panache of your new jewellery.

Enjoy!

MATERIALS + TOOLS

(Quantities listed: necklace/earrings)

4/4 Swarovski® beads, light green, ø 4 mm

5/0 Swarovski® beads, moss green, ø 6 mm

5/2 glass pearl beads, dark green, ø 6 mm

5/4 glass pearl beads, dark green, ø 4 mm

4/0 cut glass crystal cubes, light green, ø 6 mm

4/4 glass pearl cube beads, light green, ø 4 mm

2 calotte crimps

Approx. 80 crimp beads, ø 1 mm

2 end jump rings, oval

Approx. 39 in. (1 m) jewellery wire with nylon
   coating, 24 gauge (ø 0.5 mm)

1 lobster claw clasp

2 gold hoops

2 ear hooks

2 round jump rings

Jewellery glue

Round nose pliers, bent nose pliers

Side-cutting pliers

TECHNIQUE + TIPS

The secret of these pieces of jewellery is the combination of colours and shapes. The shades of colour should be chosen from one colour family. The sizes of the beads barely differ, but the shapes and kinds of beads compensate by varying considerably. When you choose your beads, do make sure that you think carefully about this so that your necklace will give you years of pleasure.

The numbers given in the list of materials show you the number of beads you will need for the earrings as well as the necklace.

THE NECKLACE

1. Use the side-cutting pliers to cut the jewellery wire into three even lengths.

2. Thread a crimp bead on to the end of each piece of wire and, using the bent nose pliers, secure it approx. ¹⁄₁₆ in. (2 mm) from the end of the wire.

3. Take the three wires, hold them together at the top and thread them together with the crimp beads into a calotte crimp. Fill the hole in the calotte crimp with a little jewellery glue, and use the round nose pliers to press it firmly closed (**illustration a**).

4. You should now have three wires of the same length that are attached at one end.

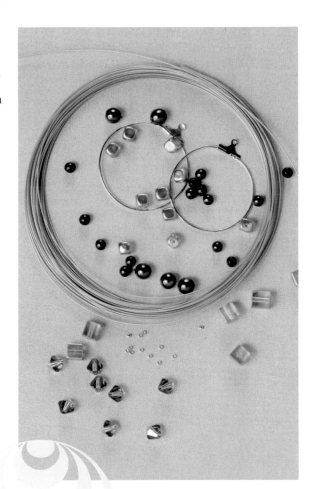

5. Start to string the beads. Begin by threading the first wire, making sure that you alternate the shape and kind of beads. Before and after every bead, thread on a crimp bead and fix it carefully into place using the bent nose pliers. The distance between the beads should vary between about ¾ in. (2 cm) and 3 in. (8 cm). This will make the necklace look particularly attractive.

6. Once you have threaded the first wire, thread the other wires in exactly the same way. As you work, make sure you offset the beads to give the necklace a casual look.

7. Cut all the wires to exactly the same length, and, as you did in Step 5, thread a crimp bead ⅟₁₆ in. (2 mm) from the end of each wire and squeeze it firmly together.

8. Twist the wires gently over each other so that they look as if they're joined together.

9. Now push the three ends of wire and the crimp beads into the second calotte crimp, fill it with a little jewellery glue, and squeeze the calotte crimp together with the pliers.

10. Finally, secure an oval jump ring to each calotte crimp, and insert the lobster claw clasp into one of the jump rings before closing it.

THE EARRINGS

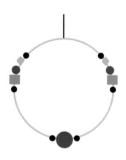

1. Take one of the hoops and thread the beads in the following sequence: crimp bead, light green Swarovski® bead (4 mm), dark green glass pearl (4 mm), light green glass pearl cube (4 mm), 2 crimp beads, dark green glass pearl (6 mm), 2 crimp beads, light green glass pearl cube (4 mm), dark green glass pearl (4 mm), light green Swarovski® bead (4 mm), crimp bead.

2. Fix the crimp beads in the places shown (in black) on the diagram on the left. You can, of course, choose to position the beads wherever you like. Then close the hoop.

3. Open a jump ring by bending one side of the ring towards your body and the other away from you. Slip the ear hook and hoop on to the jump ring, then close it again.

4. Repeat all the steps to make the second earring.

Glass bead necklace with earrings   37

Charm bracelet

■ ■ □

MATERIALS + TOOLS

4–6 in. (10–15 cm) cable chain
   (brass/silver-plated)

Approx. 30 head pins, silver-plated

2 end jump rings, silver-plated

30 round jump rings, silver-plated, ø 5 mm

Glass and seed beads of your choice

1 lobster claw clasp

Side-cutting pliers

Bent nose pliers

Round nose pliers

TECHNIQUE + TIPS

First, measure the circumference of your wrist, then shorten the cable chain to the right length using side-cutting pliers. Make sure you also include the length of the clasp. Arrange the beads in size order. Then lay out the cable chain on the work surface and position the beads in the order you like best. The bracelet should be richly loaded. The 'charms' are attached using head pins that you cut to different lengths using the side-cutting pliers.

1. First, fill the individual head pins with the beads of your choice. Begin with the long head pins and thread several beads on to them. About 10–12 long head pins with beads should be enough.

2. Make sure you leave at least ⅓ in. (1 cm) of the head pin clear to allow you to make a closed loop later.

3. Take 10–12 shorter head pins and fill them with one large or several small beads. Again you must leave ⅓ in. (1 cm) of the head pin clear. If necessary, shorten the head pins to the right length using the side-cutting pliers.

4. Once all the head pins are filled with beads, it is time to form the loops. If you are right-handed, hold the head pin firmly in your left hand while using the round nose pliers to form a loop with your right hand. Left-handers should perform this operation the opposite way round. This may sound rather complicated, but will become much easier with a little practice (**illustration a**).

5. Now link each of the loops you've just made on the head pins into a jump ring. Then link the jump rings attached to the head pins into the flat links on the cable chain. Do make sure that you maintain the same distances between the rings, and only link the jump rings into flat links on the chain, so that the bracelet doesn't twist afterwards (**illustrations b + c**).

6. Repeat Step 5 with the shorter head pins, securing them between the longer head pins. Again, remember to space them evenly! Finally, attach end jump rings at each end of the cable chain and insert the clasp.

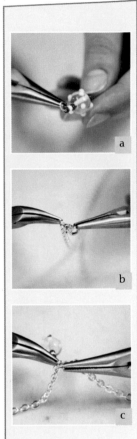

It's easy to make matching earrings using head pins and ear hooks.

MATERIALS + TOOLS

2 packets of Colour Melt Crystals, transparent

Approx. 9 in. (23 cm) cable chain

Approx. 30 jump rings, ø 7 mm

7 moulds for melting the crystals, ø 1½ in. (4 cm)

1 sheet (size A4) aluminium sheet for embossing

1 lobster claw clasp

Scissors

Skewers or knitting needle

2 pairs of round nose pliers

Drill with thinnest drill bit

Washing-up pad

TECHNIQUE + TIPS

You can get nickel-free materials in any craft shop. Materials from general stockists often contain nickel and can trigger allergies.

1. Fill the moulds three-quarters full with the crystals, and bake them in the oven at 350°F (180°C) for approx. 30 minutes. Leave to cool, then file off the burrs. Scour the discs with the abrasive side of the washing-up pad to give them a matt finish. Then, using a slow drill speed, drill a hole in each disc approx. 1/16 in. (2 mm) from the edge. Using the round nose pliers, attach a jump ring into each hole. Then link another ring into the first so that the discs will be able to move freely. Attach the last ring to each alternating flat link of the cable chain. Each alternate flat link remains empty.

2. Take 6 moulds, half-fill them with crystals, and repeat the procedure for making the discs as in Step 1. Create a heart shape out of paper, lay it on the aluminium sheet, and emboss the shape on to the metal using the skewer. Cut out six hearts and lay each one in a mould. Fill the moulds with crystals, melt them for 30 minutes at 350°F (180°C), then allow them to cool. File off the burrs, drill a hole into the edge of each disc 1/16 in. (2 mm) from the edge, and link them into the remaining flat links on the cable chain. Attach the clasp with a jump ring.

Anklet with hearts   43

Flower ring with garnets and Murano glass

■ ■ □

MATERIALS + TOOLS

4 garnet beads

Murano glass beads of your choice

Glass bead selection in shades of green

Stainless steel ring in your size with
  'sieve' for head pins

Approx. 18 head pins, silver, ¾ in. (2 cm)

Round nose pliers

Side-cutting pliers

TECHNIQUE + TIPS

This ring is a real eye-catcher. Because of the garnets and the different types of beads it looks like a wonderful bunch of flowers and, despite its size, it is very easy to wear. When arranging the individual beads, make sure they look good together. Thread the larger beads on first – this way they'll sit uppermost on the ring – and thread the small or flat beads over them.

1. First, unscrew the sieve from the ring to allow you to insert the individual head pins.

2. Now take the head pins and fill them with the individual beads. You should thread two or three different kinds and colours of bead on to each head pin. Use the large beads first, followed by the small ones. The flat end of each head pin will now look like the head of a nail.

3. Starting at the middle, push the head pins one after the other through the holes in the sieve. Make sure you create a good overall impression of shapes and flowers.

4. Push the head pins firmly through the holes using the round nose pliers, and bend the ends over into rings. If necessary you can shorten the head pins with the side-cutting pliers first.

5. Bend the rings over using the round nose pliers and press them flat against the base of the sieve.

6. Once you have filled all the holes in the sieve with the head pins and bent over all the rings, screw the sieve back on to the ring.

Crystal ball pendant

■ ■ ■

MATERIALS + TOOLS

Approx. 39 in. (1 m) nylon thread, 30 gauge
   (ø 0.25 mm)

Approx. 12 in. (30 cm) silicon cord,
   18 gauge (ø approx. 1 mm)

30 cut glass crystal beads (here red), ø 4–6 mm

2 calotte crimps (for the silicon cord)

1 clasp, e.g. lobster claw, 2 end jump rings

Jewellery glue, small round nose pliers

TECHNIQUE + TIPS

The crystal ball is a real showpiece. Making it requires skill and patience.
It's best to practise the technique first. Once you've understood the
principle, you'll be sure to use it over and over again, as the balls have all
sorts of uses: as pendants, ring jewellery, earrings or mobile phone dangles.

The important thing to remember is that the nylon thread on to which the
beads are strung is fed through the last bead and the one next to it one
more time at the end to strengthen the ball. The larger the ball becomes,
the fewer new beads are threaded on to each ring, each of which is made
up of five beads.

The numerous photos and diagrams show the individual steps. Look at
them carefully.

> For the five inner bead rings string
> on the following number of new
> beads per ring:
> 4 – 3 – 3 – 3 – 2
> The number of new beads per ring
> for the outer five bead rings is:
> 3 – 2 – 2 – 2 – 1

1. First, thread two beads on to the nylon
   thread. Position the beads in the centre
   of the thread and cross the thread
   through the fifth bead. If you would
   like to fix the beads more securely you
   can tie a knot here (**illustrations a**).

2. Now string four more beads and take
   the thread back through the first bead
   of the first ring again. Now you have
   two rings (**illustrations b**).

This photograph shows what you can do with the crystal bead ball. You can make it using one or more colours, and use it as a pendant or earring, or mount it on a ring.

'The best way to cheer yourself up is to try to cheer somebody else up.'

Mark Twain

c

d

e

f

g

3. Continue to repeat Step 2 until you have created a total of four rings around the centre ring. For the closing fifth circle you only need to thread on two new beads (**illustrations c + d**).

4. Now you've almost got half a ball (**illustration e**). The ball is completed by adding a further five rings to your existing beadwork. From now on you will use fewer beads in each ring.

5. Take the left thread and pass it through the bead next to it. Put three new beads on to the right thread. Now take the left thread and pass it through the third bead of the new row. This gives you another new ring consisting of five beads (**illustration f**).

6. You make the next two rings in exactly the same way, but only thread two new beads on to each new ring (**illustration f**).

7. To form the fifth ring you only use one bead. Make sure you always remember to thread through the next bead in the existing bead rings (**illustration f**).

8. Now you'll find that a ball forms almost by itself. All you need to do now is to pull the threads from both sides through the bottom five beads, knot the ends and secure the knots with a little jewellery glue (**illustration g**).

9. Pull the silicon cord through the ball, reinforce each end with a calotte crimp, and, using two pairs of round nose pliers, fix on the jump rings and clasp.

Double hoop earrings with mother-of-pearl discs

■ □ □

MATERIALS + TOOLS

2 double hoop components, outside
ø approx. 1 in. (2.5 cm), each with
5 rings

12 jump rings, silver, ø 5 mm

12 mother-of-pearl discs, light green with
1 hole, ø ½ in. (1.5 cm)

Round nose pliers
Bent nose pliers

TECHNIQUE + TIPS

You can buy double hoop components
with pre-formed loops from larger craft
suppliers. This makes it easy to create
unusual and individual earrings to suit
your personal taste. Don't worry if you're
only able to get single hoop components;
they'll be fine too. The reason we
recommend the double hoops is we think
they look more effective!

'Even a journey of a
thousand miles begins
with a single step.'

Japanese proverb

1. Bend open the 12 jump rings using the
   round nose pliers and bent nose pliers.
   Don't forget to bend one side of the
   ring towards your body and the other
   away. This prevents the basic shape of
   the ring from being deformed.

2. Now put a jump ring through the hole
   in each of the mother-of-pearl discs,
   then link the jump rings into the
   double hoop component.

3. Close the jump rings using both sets
   of pliers.

Name bracelet with Swarovski® beads

■ ■ ■

MATERIALS + TOOLS

Approx. 39 in. (1 m) nylon thread, 30 gauge
  (ø 0.25 mm)

9 Swarovski® beads, orange, ø 4 mm

12 Swarovski® beads, moss green, ø 4 mm

10 Swarovski® beads, salmon pink, ø 4 mm

12 Swarovski® beads, wine red, ø 4 mm

9 Swarovski® beads, amber, ø 4 mm

12 Swarovski® beads, soft pink, ø 6 mm

5 glass letter beads of your choice

1 screw clasp, jewellery glue

TECHNIQUE + TIPS

You can change the name bracelet – depending on the length of the name – by making more bead rings and shortening the bead row at the end. Don't forget to measure the circumference of your wrist first!

Our bracelet is about 7 in. (18 cm) long, including the screw clasp; each bead ring measures just over ½ in. (approx. 1.5 cm).

Instead of letters you can also use gemstones with other motifs – another opportunity to give your creativity free rein!

The important thing about this technique is that you begin by making the first bead ring. The bead chain that leads from the first ring to the clasp is added right at the end.

The choice of colours is completely up to you. We chose colourful stones for this piece of jewellery. However, all the beads within one ring should be one colour.

You'll find the instructions for making the bracelet on the next page. Have lots of fun making your personal message!

This is how you start: pass the thread through the eight beads, then string the L, reversed left to right, onto both threads. Push it to the centre of the bead ring and turn it over. You don't need to worry about this with symmetrical letters.

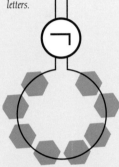

Carry on like this: push the L into the bead ring, then flip it over. Pass the left thread back through the four beads on the left side, and the right thread through the beads on the right, making a double knot at the end.

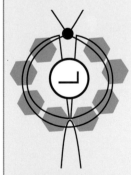

This is how you finish off: pass the second thread through the thread linking the first bead ring and string the beads on to both threads.

1. Start with the first bead ring, in our example the one with the L. Cut 31½ in. (80 cm) off the nylon thread and thread eight orange Swarovski® beads on to the centre. Then thread the L, reversed left to right, on to both threads, pull the gemstone with the L into the centre of the bead ring, and turn it over. The threads are now underneath and the L is the right way up.

2. Pass the left thread back though the four beads on the left, and the right thread back through the four beads on the right, so that they both finish up at the top. Close the bead ring with a double knot.

3. Now string one of the 6 mm beads on to both threads.

4. Repeat Steps 1 to 3 for each bead ring. With symmetrical symbols or letters you don't need to worry about threading the gemstone on reversed left to right. For each bead ring select the bead colour of your choice. We chose orange, moss green, salmon pink, wine red and amber as our colour sequence.

5. Once you have made all the bead rings, bring both threads together after the last double knot, then thread on large and small Swarovski® beads in an alternating sequence.

6. The length of the string of beads depends on the number of bead rings and the circumference of your wrist. We threaded on five small and four large beads in alternating order. Use three small Swarovski® beads in wine red to finish the bead chain.

7. Now take one part of the screw clasp and knot both ends of the thread through the jump ring on the end. Pass the ends of the thread back through the last bead, cut the end off cleanly, and fix the knot at the clasp with a little jewellery glue.

8. All that's missing is the second string of beads. Take the remains of the nylon thread – 8 in. (20 cm)–and pass it through the thread linking the first bead ring, as illustrated below left.

9. The next step is to string the beads on to both threads following the same sequence as you used for the first string of beads.

10. Finally, take the second part of the screw clasp and knot the ends of the thread through the jump ring.

Antique necklace

MATERIALS + TOOLS

Approx. 40 antique jump rings, ø 7 mm

Approx. 14 antique head pins, 0.7 × 35 mm

3 antique jewellery pendants, 16 × 23 mm

Approx. 20 glass pearls, rust brown, ø 10 mm

Approx. 20 glass pearls, mother-of-pearl, ø 70 mm

Approx. 10 g seed beads, brown with silver inside,
    ø 2.6 mm

Approx. 10 g seed beads, honey, pearlized
    (shimmer like dragonfly wings), ø 2.6 mm

Approx. 20 cut glass crystal beads, clear, ø 6 mm

10–15 cut glass crystal beads, black, ø 6 mm

Approx. 20 Murano glass beads in pinky brown
    shades, ø 12 mm

Approx. 10 antique beads with Swarovski® stones,
    ø 8 mm

Approx. 39 in. (1 m) antique cable chain, fluted,
    ø 1.2 mm

Approx 5 ft. (1.5 m) jewellery wire (brass with
    nylon coating)

2 oval glass beads, length approx. 20 mm

Approx. 25 antique crimp beads, ø 1.4–2 mm

Jewellery glue

Side-cutting pliers

Round nose pliers

Bent nose pliers

TECHNIQUE + TIPS

The necklace is made from individual pieces, which are assembled symmetrically from the back to the front. Each piece has to be made in duplicate, apart from the front piece with the three antique jewellery pendants and the back part with the beads. All the parts – the strings of beads and the cable chain – are linked using jump rings.

1. Arrange the beads and use the side-cutting pliers to cut pieces approximately 4¾ in. (12 cm) long from the jewellery wire and cable chain. Use the round nose pliers to form a small loop at one end of every piece of jewellery wire, and secure it with a crimp bead.

2. String the individual beads according to your own personal preference. You have to thread between one and three seed beads in between the large beads so that the chain remains flexible. Remember that you will have to make each part twice!

3. Leave approx. ½ in. (1 cm) free at the end. Form a loop and secure it with a crimp bead and jewellery glue. Attach jump rings to the loops. You'll use these later to attach bead strings and cable chains.

4. Now make the single piece at the neck. You should select particularly attractive beads for this. Secure the first pair of bead strings to each end of the neck piece, then a piece of cable chain, then another bead string, and so on. You should finish with a bead string.

5. The front part of the necklace is made up of three antique jewellery pendants, to each one of which you attach three head pins, each threaded with 11 brown/silver seed beads. Again leave just over ⅓ in. (1 cm) free at the end, form a ring, and secure the head pins to the pendants using jump rings.

6. For the two pieces between the pendants, thread one oval glass bead and two mother-of-pearl beads on to each piece of wire, form the ends into loops, and secure them with a crimp bead. Finally, join together the last pair of bead strings and the jewellery pendants using the jump rings.

Dragonfly hair comb

MATERIALS + TOOLS

Aluminium embossing sheet, 4 × 4 in. (10 × 10 cm)

Thin leather, black, 8 × 8 in. (20 × 20 cm)

1 plastic hair comb, black, approx. 2¾ in. (7 cm) wide

Approx. 20 in. (50 cm) jewellery wire, silver

12 crimp beads

6 Swarovski® jewellery pendants with 2 holes, 8 × 4 mm

10 Swarovski® stones, self-adhesive or iron-on, ø 5 mm

Approx. 50 Swarovski® stones, self-adhesive or iron-on, ø 4 mm

Approx. 60 Swarovski® stones, self-adhesive or iron-on, ø 3 mm

Sewing needle, side-cutting pliers, round nose pliers, bent nose pliers, dressmaking scissors, tin snips, jewellery glue

Nails, hammer, a piece of felt ½ in. (1 cm) thick, waterproof felt-tipped pen

TECHNIQUE + TIPS

This striking hair comb also requires a lot of skill. Be careful when using the tin snips and heating up the needle – you should use pliers with rubber handles when handling the hot needle. Work slowly and carefully! If you don't like the colour black you can, of course, choose shades of brown or other colours. Just make sure the comb and leather go together.

1. Draw two different-sized dragonflies on to paper and cut both shapes out. You will find a pattern on page 58.

2. Lay the shapes on the tin sheet and draw the dragonflies on to the tin using the waterproof felt-tipped pen (**illustration a**).

3. Cut the shapes out of the tin sheet using the tin snips (**illustration b**). Be careful when using them!

4. Cut the piece of leather into four squares. Brush the rough side of the leather with jewellery glue (**illustration c**).

5. Place each tin dragonfly on one of the pieces of leather so that they adhere to the glue.

6. Take the other two pieces of leather, and with the glued surface facing downwards, press them firmly down on to the dragonflies. The tin sheet is now covered with leather on both sides.

7. Press the dragonflies firmly together. Ideally, leave them overnight under a pile of books to allow the glue to dry properly.

8. Take your fabric scissors, and cut the finished dragonfly out, cutting approximately 1 mm from the edge of the tin sheet (**illustration d**). You can feel and see where the tin sheet ends. The tin sheet is easy to see under the thin leather. That aside, you would find it hard to cut through the tin sheet with the fabric scissors.

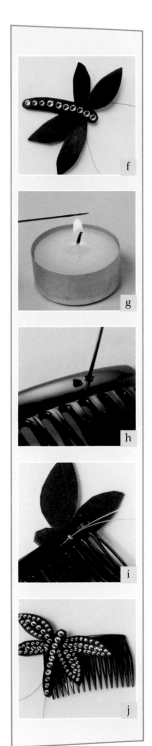

'The secret of success is constancy of purpose.'

Benjamin Disraeli

9. Lay the dragonflies on the felt and use the hammer to carefully make two holes at the front of the body (**illustration e**, page 57).

10. Now you can iron on the Swarovski® stones. Use the larger stones for the body and inner edge of the wings. Place a line of smaller stones at the outside edge of the wings (**illustration f**).

11. Take the sewing needle, grip it firmly with the round nose pliers, and heat it over a candle. Using the hot tip of the needle, melt two holes in the edge of each comb. The two holes should be ⅛ in. (4 mm) away from each other (**illustrations g + h**).

12. Cut two pieces of jewellery wire measuring approx. 8–10 in. (20–25 cm). Thread each piece of wire down through the dragonfly, then through one of the holes in the comb.

13. Thread a crimp bead on to each wire protruding from the underside of the comb and squeeze it firmly together directly underneath. The comb and dragonfly should now be firmly attached to each other. Repeat the procedure with the other dragonfly (**illustration i**).

14. Now you can thread the Swarovski® jewellery pendants on to the wire in your preferred order and at varying distances apart, fixing the pendants on both sides with a crimp bead (**illustration j**).

15. Finally, cut off the ends of the wires immediately after the last crimp bead.

Swarovski® earrings

MATERIALS + TOOLS

2 ear hooks, silver

6 eye pins, 2 in. (5 cm)

6 head pins, ¾ in. (2 cm)

6 silver beads, oval, 6 × 4 mm

16 Swarovski® beads, amber,
   ø 4 mm

14 Swarovski® beads, orange,
   ø 4 mm

14 Swarovski® beads, salmon,
   ø 4 mm

10 Swarovski® beads, wine-red,
   ø 4 mm

14 jump rings, silver, ø 5 mm

Approx. 6 in. (15 cm) cable chain, silver,
   ø 4 × 3 mm

Side-cutting pliers

Bent nose pliers

Round nose pliers

TECHNIQUE + TIPS

These earrings are made up of three lots of three individual pieces that, despite their amazing appearance, are just so easy to make. Do you know yet on which special occasion you're going to choose to wear your earrings, or which clothes you would like to wear to go with them? That's good, because the colours you choose can depend on your choice of clothes – again, it's your decision. Check that the colours match though! When buying the ear hooks, make sure that they're nickel-free.

1. Start with the longest string of beads. Take an eye pin and thread ten of the Swarovski® beads on to it in an alternating colour sequence.

2. You must always leave approx. ½ in. (1 cm) at the end of each eye pin. If necessary, use the side-cutting pliers to shorten the eye pin to this length. Form a closed loop at this end using the bent nose pliers. Repeat Steps 1 and 2 with the second earring.

3. For the medium-length bead string, thread eight Swarovski® beads, shorten the surplus end of the eye pin to ½ in. (1 cm), and again form a closed loop at the end. Repeat this step with the second earring.

4. All that's missing is the shortest bead string. To make this, thread six Swarovski® beads on to the eye pin, shorten the end to ½ in. (1 cm), and form a closed loop. Likewise, repeat this step with the second earring.

5. To make each earring take a long, medium and short bead string. Bend one of the jump rings open, by bending one side of the ring towards you and the other away from your body. Now link the three bead strings by their loops into the jump ring, close it up again, and suspend it from the ear hook.

6. Now cut the cable chain into six equal lengths. Alternatively you can bend open the rings in the cable chain, then close them again. We used seven rings for each earring.

7. Take two jump rings for each piece of cable chain, open them, and insert them into the first and last links of the cable chain. Link one bead chain into one of the jump rings and close this jump ring using the round nose pliers.

8. Now thread a Swarovski® bead and a silver bead on to each head pin. Bend the end of the head pin into a closed loop.

9. Link this loop into the open jump ring at the end of the cable chain, then close this jump ring too. Repeat this step for each piece.

MATERIALS + TOOLS

1 packet of Colour Melt Crystals, orange

4 moulds, ø 2¾ in (7 cm)

8 moulds, ø 1½ in. (4 cm)

1 clip clasp

6 Scoubidou strings, orange

13 2-hole jewellery beads, square, 8 × 8 mm;
  we have used enamelled metal beads in
  pink, orange and cream

Approx. 12 in. (30 cm) aluminium strip

Jewellery glue

Drill with fine drill bit

File

Scissors

Washing-up pad

TECHNIQUE + TIPS

Make sure the side of the crystal disc that was to the inside of the mould during the solidifying process is now to the outside. This side has a smoother surface. The length of the hip chain can be altered by changing the length of the Scoubidou string. If required you can vary it by changing the distance between the individual discs.

1. Half fill the eight small moulds with crystals. Then cut the aluminium strip into equal-sized squares and place one piece in each of the four large moulds. Fill the larger moulds half full with crystals round the aluminium square. Now you have four moulds with a square hole in the middle.

2. Make small tubes out of aluminium and position them in the moulds to keep holes clear while the crystals melt in the oven. You need four holes per disc (see photograph opposite and diagram overleaf). Place all the moulds in the oven at 350°F (180°C) for about 30 minutes, then leave them to cool. Now file off the burrs and roughen the surface with the abrasive side of the washing-up pad.

3. Take 2 Scoubidou strings, measure approx. 8 in. (20 cm) along each of them, and start the belt here. Loop a simple knot into each string and thread the long ends, from above, into the holes in one of the large discs.

4. Now thread both strings through one of the beads, crossing the strings as you do so, and securing the bead in the centre of the square hole.

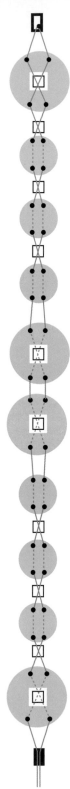

Clip counterpart

Fastener and 8 in. (20 cm) strings. Another two small crystal discs and two beads will be knotted onto here.

5. Thread the strings from below through the other two holes and knot them, so that the crystal disc is also fixed in place.

6. Now thread a jewellery bead crosswise on to both strings.

7. The next step is to thread on one of the small crystal discs. Always make sure you knot the strings to prevent the individual pieces from slipping.

8. The diagram on the left shows you the order in which you should thread the individual pieces. Each black dot symbolizes a knot, and each black-edged square a jewellery bead. The dotted lines indicate that the strings should run behind the disc.

9. If a Scoubidou string isn't long enough, just tie a new one on to it. This will look best if you make sure that the knot is behind one of the discs. Fix the knots with jewellery glue.

Also make sure the string always runs underneath the crystal discs and is knotted at the top. As the steps are all repeated you quickly get into a pattern.

10. Now it's time for the clip fastener: knot both parts of the fastener on to the strings. Then use the 8 in. (20 cm) lengths of string that remain for the jewellery piece at the front. Thread a bead, a small disc, another bead, another small disc and finally a bead just as it shows you in the photo, and in exactly the same way as you're used to.

11. All you need to do now is knot the strings, cut off the ends and secure the knots with jewellery glue.

'Arabian Nights' anklet

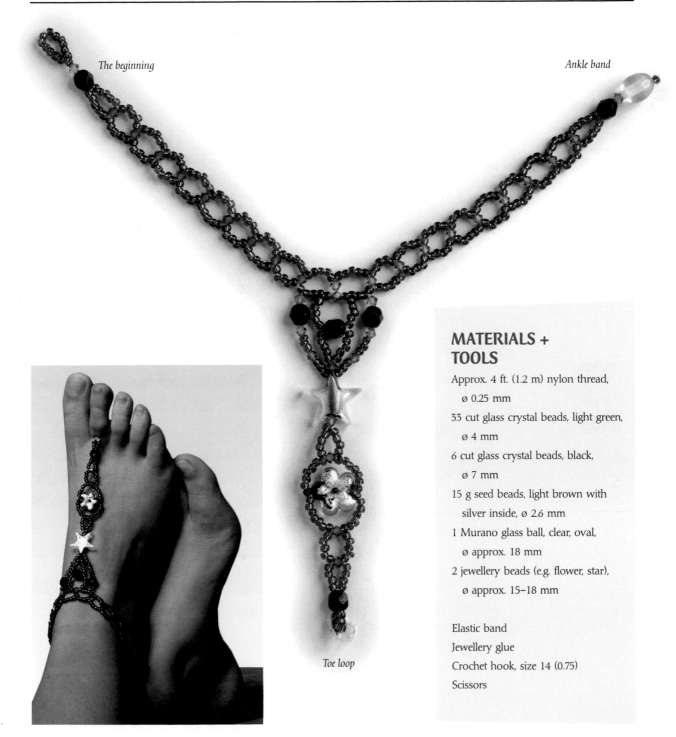

The beginning

Ankle band

Toe loop

MATERIALS + TOOLS

Approx. 4 ft. (1.2 m) nylon thread,
ø 0.25 mm

33 cut glass crystal beads, light green,
ø 4 mm

6 cut glass crystal beads, black,
ø 7 mm

15 g seed beads, light brown with
silver inside, ø 2.6 mm

1 Murano glass ball, clear, oval,
ø approx. 18 mm

2 jewellery beads (e.g. flower, star),
ø approx. 15–18 mm

Elastic band
Jewellery glue
Crochet hook, size 14 (0.75)
Scissors

TECHNIQUE + TIPS

You do need to pay a lot of attention to the example, but it's not as complicated as it first looks. The ring pattern is perfect for this kind of jewellery, because it is not only elastic and flexible, but also sturdy. An important thing to remember is that you must make an even number of rings for the chain round the ankle. In our example we worked with 20 rings, which correspond to a length of about 10¼ in. (26 cm). Measure the circumference of your ankle (not too tightly!), and calculate how many rings you will need for the ankle chain.

1. We start with the chain that goes round the ankle. Take approx. 24 in. (60 cm) nylon thread, find the middle, and thread 12 seed beads on to the centre. Now take a 13th bead and pass both threads – one from the left, one from the right – through it. You repeat this with one of the green and one of the black beads.

2. Now separate out the two threads again; on to each of them thread five brown seed beads. Next, take a green cut glass crystal bead and again string both threads from both sides through it.

3. Repeat Step 2 until you have made the required number of rings; in our example we made 20.

4. The last ring is closed first with a black, then a green bead. After the green bead thread the large Murano glass bead as a fastener. Now thread on another seed bead, knot the ends of the thread, hide them inside the last bead, and fix them with jewellery glue.

This diagram shows you the exact order of the beads and how to thread them. Use this as a pattern.

Ankle chain

Toe loop

This is how you start: this photo shows how the rings for the ankle chain are beaded.

5. Next, start on the piece that leads down to your toes. You have to count well here! Divide the rest of the nylon thread into two even lengths. Take the two centre rings of the ankle chain and pass the first thread through the four inside seed beads of the two rings. Secure it with another green bead. String the beads on to both ends of the thread, as shown in the photo below.

6. Feed the second thread through the new green and two brown beads on either side of it. Now string five seed beads on to each side.

7. It is best to look at the diagram on the left to see how the threads are beaded and what the pattern looks like. The important thing is that after the star you should feed two threads through each bead. This gives it added strength. The ends of the four threads are knotted, stuck into the beads and secured with jewellery glue.

8. To make the toe loop, fold the elastic band double, crochet a row of chain stitches in the middle, and knot the ends into the last bead ring.

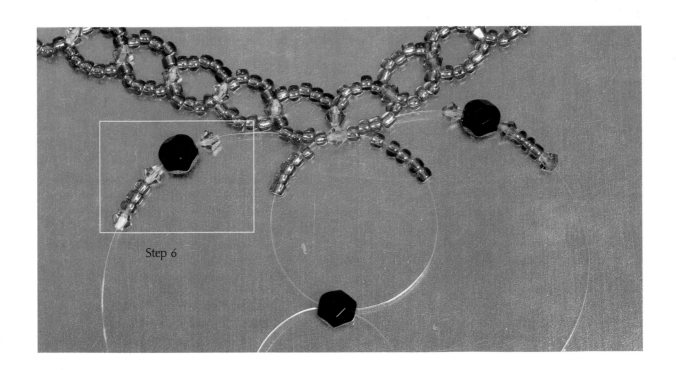

Step 6

Blue bead necklace

MATERIALS + TOOLS

Approx. 5 ft. (1.5 m) jewellery wire, silver,
   with nylon coating, 30 gauge
   (ø 0.25 mm)

Approx. 50 Murano glass beads in various
   shapes and sizes, blue colours of your
   choice

Seed beads

Small silver beads (quantity according
   to taste)

1 calotte crimp, ø 2 mm

1 crimp bead, silver, ø 1.4 mm

1 crimp bead, silver, ø 2.0 mm

1 lobster claw clasp, 1 cm

2 oval jump rings, ø 4 mm

Side–cutting pliers, bent nose pliers

Round nose pliers

TECHNIQUE + TIPS

This chain is very easy to make and can be made highly individual. In our example we have chosen different shades of blue and silver. If you prefer shades of red or perhaps earthy tones, you can, of course, choose a different combination. But do make sure you only choose colours from the same colour family, otherwise the chain will be too gaudy. It's also up to you to decide what length necklace you'd like.

1. Take the jewellery wire and thread the beads on to it at varying distances apart. We chose distances of about ¾ in.–1½ in. (2–4 cm).

2. It's quite easy to fix the beads into place on the jewellery wire: thread the bead into its chosen position, then run the end of the wire round the outside of the bead and back in through the bead again. The wire will now hold the bead in this position.

3. Vary the shade of colour, shape and size of the beads so that you create a bit of variety. Thread smaller glass beads or seed beads in between, too.

4. When the necklace is the right length, it's time to fit the clasp.

5. Take one end of the jewellery wire and thread the calotte crimp on to it. Press it together using the round nose pliers to secure it.

6. Now take one of the oval jump rings and bend it open. Use the round nose pliers and bent nose pliers, and remember to bend one end towards your body and the other away from you. Finally, link the jump ring into the ring on the calotte crimp and close it again.

7. Thread the smaller, then the larger, crimp bead on to the other end of the jewellery wire. Shape the surplus end of the wire into a loop, lead it back through both crimp beads, and press them together using the round nose pliers. Take the second jump ring, bend it apart, feed it through this loop, through the ring of the lobster clasp, and close it carefully.

Ring with cultured pearls and garnets

TECHNIQUE + TIPS

The cultured pearls and choice of colours make this ring look very sophisticated and unusual. At the same time it is easy and uncomplicated to make.

MATERIALS + TOOLS

Approx. 10 g garnet chips

Approx. 10 g pink cultured pearls

Approx. 10 g white cultured pearls

20 in. (50 cm) nylon-covered rubber
   thread, 30 gauge (ø 0.25 mm)

Jewellery glue

Sewing needle

Wooden baton (e.g. hammer handle)

'You never know what will happen if things are changed. But who knows what will happen if they're not changed?'

Elias Canetti

1. Take the rubberized thread and tie a knot at one end, so that the pearls don't slide off.

2. Now thread the three types of bead on to the thread, preferably at random (**illustration a**).

3. As you work, make sure you check the length every so often. Once you can twist the string of pearls round your chosen finger three and a half times – without stretching it – it's the right length.

4. Take a wooden baton to help you form your ring. We used a hammer handle.

5. Take the string of beads, secure the end with a knot, and fix into place on the wooden handle using a strip of glue.

6. Now wind the string of beads round the handle (**illustration b**).

7. Once you have wound the beads completely round the handle, thread the end of the rubberized thread into a sewing needle and sew through the individual rows of beads in a zigzag pattern. This weaves the rows of beads together.

8. Thread the needle over and under the rows of beads until you're back at the beginning (**illustration c**).

9. Now knot the two ends of the thread, cut the surplus ends off, and secure the knot with a little jewellery glue. Finally, tuck the knot under the beads.

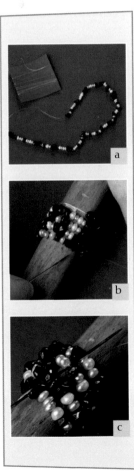

Ring with cultured pearls and garnets

Oriental bracelet

MATERIALS + TOOLS

7 jewellery components, antique brass,
with 4 holes, 16 × 11 mm

7 cut glass crystal beads, black, ø 7 mm

70 cut glass crystal beads, honey, pearlized,
ø 4 mm

Approx. 39 in. (1 m) nylon covered elastic
cord (Stretch Magic), 30 gauge (ø 0.25 mm)

Jewellery glue

TECHNIQUE + TIPS

This bracelet is incredibly effective, yet at the same time not
as complicated to make as it looks. The pattern repeats itself
over and over again. The flexibility of the elastic cord means
you don't need any kind of clasp. All you need to do is to
knot the ends. An important tip: use glue strips to secure the
ends of the rubber threads to your work surface.

1. Separate the elastic cord into two even lengths and use glue strips to fix them next to each other on your work surface.

2. Start with the first pattern: string two each of the honey crystal beads on to each of the threads.

3. Next, feed both threads through one of the 7 mm black crystal beads. Cross the two threads over: the one from the right continues on the left and vice versa.

4. String two more honey crystal beads on to each of the two threads.

5. Now it's time for the antique jewellery component: lead the threads down through the first hole on either side of the jewellery piece, then back up through the second hole.

6. String a honey crystal bead on to each of the two threads and feed each thread back through both holes in the piece of jewellery as described in Step 5.

7. You have now finished the first pattern. Repeat Steps 2–6 until your bracelet is the right length for your wrist.

8. Finish off your beading with an antique jewellery component. Then take the ends of the elastic cords that you had secured with the glue strips at the beginning, and knot them with the ends of the cords leading through the bracelet.

9. Cut off the surplus ends and fix the knot with a little jewellery glue.

Turquoise necklace with satin tie

MATERIALS + TOOLS

5 furry pom-poms, turquoise

Approx. 12 antique-look metal beads, silver

2 satin beads, turquoise, ø 1 in. (2 cm)

2 bead-covered beads, pearlized, black

15 glass beads, turquoise, mixed, ø 4–7 mm

2 cut glass crystal beads, anthracite, ø 1 in. (2.5 cm)

3 real turquoises

1 antique-look toggle clasp, silver

5 ft (1.5 m) satin ribbon, turquoise, ⅓ in.
   (9 mm) wide

1 heart-shaped jewellery pendant, 9 mm wide

5 cut glass crystal beads, black, ø 6 mm

5 cut glass crystal beads, clear, ø 10 mm

5 ft. (1.5 m) jewellery wire, silver

Crimp beads

Jewellery glue, sewing needle, side-cutting pliers,
   round nose pliers

TECHNIQUE + TIPS

Because this necklace is quite heavy, it is particularly important to make it strong. So that there are no weak points, we have used a special technique, whereby the jewellery wire is always threaded through the beads twice. A loop of jewellery wire is made for the pom-poms so that they can be threaded on to the double-thickness jewellery wire.

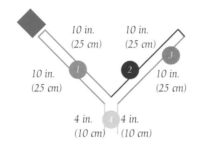

1. Prepare the pom-poms for threading on to the jewellery wire. Take 12 in. (30 cm) of the wire and cut it into five even lengths using the side-cutting pliers (**illustration a**).

2. Thread a piece of wire on to the sewing needle, and pull the wire through the pom-pom twice to make a loop. Pull the loop as tight as possible. You must make sure the loop is big enough to accommodate the double thickness of jewellery wire, but tight enough for the pom-pom to sit firmly on the necklace. Repeat for the other four pom-poms.

3. Thread crimp beads on to both ends of the wire on each pom-pom and secure them firmly against the pom-pom using bent nose pliers. Cut the surplus ends off using the side-cutting pliers.

4. Now you can start to thread up the necklace. Take the remaining wire. Look carefully at the diagram (above); it shows you how to bend the wire and the order in which you need to string the beads.

5. Start with the piece of wire marked green in the diagram. Measure a length of 14 in. (35 cm) from the end of the wire and bend the wire over at this point. Loop one half of the satin ribbon round the wire (**illustration b**).

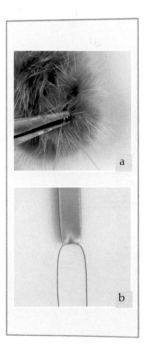

6. Thread one of the turquoise-coloured small glass beads over both ends of the wire and push it tightly up to the satin ribbon (**illustration c**).

7. Thread the other beads on one after the other in your chosen sequence. What you must remember to do every so often is insert one or more of the small beads so that the necklace remains flexible. Remember to thread two pom-poms on to this part of the necklace (**illustration d**).

8. When you've got about 4 in. (10 cm) left at the end of the shorter wire, separate out the ends of the wires. You don't need the shorter end yet.

9. Now take the long end of the wire and thread the beads on to it as you have already done on the other side. Remember that you're now threading 'backwards', so not from back to front any more, but vice versa. Make sure your beads are symmetrical so that your necklace looks good when it's finished.

10. Again, the last bead to be threaded before the satin ribbon should be one of the small turquoise beads.

11. Now bend the wire over, form a loop, and lead it back through the beads that you have just strung. This ensures that this row of beads is also strengthened with a double length of wire.

12. Next, take the second satin ribbon, feed it through the loop of the second string of beads, and pull the wire as taut as possible.

13. At the front of the necklace you have two lengths of wire left which are about 4 in. (10 cm) long. Thread the last pom-pom on to both wires, then begin to thread the remaining beads–apart from the heart bead.

14. As before, you should finish with one of the smaller turquoise beads. Then thread a crimp bead, bend both ends of the wire backwards into the opening of the crimp bead, and press firmly closed using the round nose pliers (**illustrations e + f**).

15. You can thread one more bead over it to cover the end.

16. Secure a round jump ring to this loop and join the two wires with the heart-shaped pendant.

17. The final step is to knot each end of the satin ribbon with one side of the toggle clasp. This is how you adjust the length of the necklace. Just leave on the surplus ends of the satin ribbon.

Heart belt

TECHNIQUE + TIPS

We have only used one heart in our belt. If you would like to make several hearts, then allow for a piece of leather and four eyelets for each one. The instructions on how to use the eyelets will be clearly explained on the packet you have bought. Any packet containing eyelets or press-studs also includes the right tool with instructions. However, we would recommend using eyelet pliers. This is easier and there is no danger of your work slipping. When you punch the holes, it is best to lay a thick piece of leather under the piece of work and press the punch pliers on to it. That makes it easier, and the cutting edge will remain sharp for a lot longer.

MATERIALS + TOOLS

2 leather cords, red, each 5 ft. (1.5 m) long,
   ⅛ in. (4 mm) wide, 1/16 in. (2 mm) thick
1 piece of leather, red, 4 × 4 in.
   (10 × 10 cm), approx. 3–4 mm thick
4 eyelets, silver, ø 5 mm

Punch pliers
Thick piece of leather as padding
Scissors or cutter
Eyelet pliers or hammer
Paper, pen

1. It is best to draw the shape of the heart in its actual size on paper first. Mark out the four places for the eyelets, and position them in the centre of the two halves of the heart.

2. Now lay the template on the red leather and cut out the heart using scissors or a cutter.

3. Lay the paper heart on the leather heart and, using the scissors, mark out the position of the eyelets. Now take the eyelets and secure them using eyelet pliers.

4. Finally, take the two leather cords and thread them through the eyelets so that the cords lie on the reverse of the heart. Knot the ends. Wear the belt slung loosely round the hips; that's how it looks best.

Red hip chain ■ ■ □

MATERIALS + TOOLS

2 packets of Colour Melt Crystals, red

10 moulds, ø 1½ in. (4 cm)

39 in. (1 m) cable chain, 14 gauge
 (ø 7.5 mm)

60 jump rings, ø 7 mm

2 jump rings for the ends of the hip chain

1 toggle clasp, 25 mm

2 pairs round nose pliers, side-cutting pliers

Drill with fine drill bit

File

Washing-up pad

TECHNIQUE + TIPS

We have stated ten moulds in the list of materials. You need a total of 30 melted crystal discs for the hip chain, so you will have to melt three lots of crystals in the oven. Of course, you could buy 30 moulds and just do one lot of melting. Depending on your waist size you can also wind the chain round; the toggle clasp can be secured to any of the rings.

1. Fill the moulds two-thirds full with melting crystals, bake them in the oven for 30 minutes at 350°F (180°C), then leave them to cool. File off the burrs, and give discs a matt finish using the abrasive side of a washing-up pad. Make a total of 30 discs.

2. Using the lowest drill speed carefully drill a hole into each disc, leaving approx. $1/16$ in. (2 mm) clearance at the edge. Using both pairs of round nose pliers, attach a jump ring into each of the holes, then link a second jump ring into the first. Don't close the second jump ring yet. Take care when opening and closing the jump rings that you don't bend them sideways, but bend one side towards your body and the other away from you. This prevents the ring from getting deformed.

3. Now take the cable chain and, using the side-cutting pliers, shorten it to the right length for you.

4. Close the second jump ring round every sixth ring of the cable chain. Make sure you always use the rings in the cable chain that are standing vertically, as is clearly shown in the photo below. This prevents the hip chain from getting twisted.

5. Using the round nose pliers, secure the jump rings for the end of the hip chain to the very last ring on the cable chain, but do not close them yet.

6. The final step is to close the end rings round the two parts of the toggle clasp.

Mobile phone beaded dangle

■■■

MATERIALS + TOOLS

Approx. 8 in. (20 cm) nylon thread,
30 gauge (0.25 mm)

12 Swarovski® crystal beads, light pink,
ø 6 mm

9 Swarovski® crystal beads, bright pink,
ø 6 mm

12 seed beads, black, ø 2.6 mm

Approx. 4 in. (10 cm) jewellery wire

2 crimp beads

Jewellery glue

Mobile phone attachment with ring for
hanging dangle (self-adhesive), black

1 lobster claw clasp, 10 mm

1 jump ring, ø approx. 6 mm

Side-cutting pliers

Small round nose pliers

TECHNIQUE + TIPS

This project is complicated at the
beginning, and we recommend that you
practise the technique first. What you
must remember in particular is to feed
the nylon thread through the beads that
link the individual rosettes together twice
– from both sides. This is the only way to
make the shape stable and it will
automatically assume the necessary
shape. Look carefully at the pictures. They
show you the path the thread has to take.

1. Secure one end of the nylon thread with a knot, then alternate four light pink Swarovski® beads with four black seed beads (illustration a).

2. Feed the thread back through two black seed beads and one light pink Swarovski® bead from the other side.

3. In alternating order, thread one bright pink Swarovski® bead, one black seed bead, a light pink Swarovski® bead, a black seed bead and one more bright pink Swarovski® bead (illustration b).

4. Now pass the thread through the two beads that are next to the section that is already held by two threads.

5. Repeat Steps 3 and 4 until you have formed a cross shape (illustration c).

6. Close the circle by passing the thread through the four outside light pink beads and the seed beads. Where the holes are between them, thread on light pink Swarovski® beads (illustration d).

7. Knot both ends of the nylon thread and secure them with jewellery glue.

8. Next, take the jewellery wire and thread it through one of the Swarovski® beads. Then thread on a crimp bead, a bright pink Swarovski® bead, followed by another crimp bead. Feed each end of the wire back through into one of the crimp beads and secure the ends in them.

9. Finally, insert a jump ring into the short loop at the end and attach the lobster clasp to the jump ring. Now close the jump ring and clip the dangle on to the attachment ring on your phone.

a

b

c

d

Mobile phone bag

MATERIALS + TOOLS

72 cut glass crystal beads, black, ø 7 mm

72 cut glass crystal beads, red, pearlized, ø 7 mm

72 cut glass crystal beads, clear, ø 7 mm

Approx. 100 cut glass crystal beads, clear, pearlized, ø 10 mm

Approx. 20 in. (50 cm) nylon thread, 24 gauge (0.5 mm)

Approx. 10 ft. (3 m) nylon thread, 30 gauge (0.25 mm)

Fabric remnant of your own choice, 4½ × 7 in. (11 × 17 cm)

Crochet thread for handle to match material

Approx. 10 in. (25 cm) iron-on Vilene, width ½ in. (1 cm)

Jewellery glue

Crochet hook, size 14 (0.75)

Sewing needle, iron, scissors

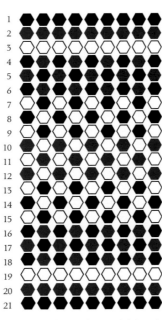

TECHNIQUE + TIPS

The mobile phone bag is made up of two separate parts: the front piece made from beads that have to be joined together very carefully to give strength, and the back part made from material that is strengthened with Vilene and given a crocheted border. The two parts are joined together using a thick nylon thread, which is sewn in – with beads – and is then also used as a handle. If you don't have enough thread for the bead weaving, simply knot on a new length and secure the knot with jewellery glue.

Pattern that can be extended depending on the size of your mobile phone.

1. Thread nine black beads on to the thin nylon thread.

2. To make the second row, string the first red bead, then draw the thread through the last black bead in the first row for a second time, again from left to right. Then you need to go back through the first red bead again, before threading the second red bead.

3. From now on, you need to join every newly threaded bead to the one directly below it in the previous row by drawing the thread through both beads. Stick closely to the pattern on the left. When you reach the end, knot the thread, tuck the end into the last bead and secure it with a little jewellery glue.

4. We recommend that right-handers turn the work after each row, facilitating beading from right to left. Left-handers should work in the opposite direction.

These photos show how to thread the beads. The end is knotted and glued.

5. That's the hardest bit done. For the back of the bag you need a piece of fabric measuring 4⅓ × 6⅔ in. (11 × 17 cm).

6. First iron in a turnover of ½ in. (1 cm) round the edge of the fabric. Lay the Vilene on top, and iron the whole thing again. Now you have a firm hem all the way round.

7. Take the crochet needle and crochet a simple lace pattern round the material, as shown in the photograph.

8. Make sure that the beads, material and crochet thread all match each other. After all, your mobile phone bag's going to be a real eye-catcher!

9. The final step is to join the bead web and the fabric. You will need the 20 in. (50 cm) length of 24 gauge (0.5 mm) nylon thread, the sewing needle and the large glass beads. You'll also be using the thread to make a handle later.

10. Lay both pieces next to each other, then thread the needle with the nylon thread, and draw it through the material. Begin with a long side. Then draw the needle through the adjoining bead and continue sewing through the beadwork and fabric as shown in the photo and diagram on the right.

11. Repeat Step 10 until the mobile phone bag is closed at the sides and bottom. The upper edge remains open of course.

12. Now all that's missing is the handle. Take the surplus end of the thick nylon thread and string the remaining large glass beads on to it. Knot the end at the other side of the bag and secure the knot with jewellery glue. The more beads you use, the longer the handle.

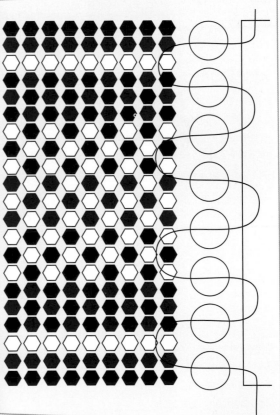

Jewellery bag

■ ■ ■

MATERIALS + TOOLS

1 skein felting wool, bright blue

½ skein felting wool, wine red

¼ skein felting wool, natural white

¼ skein felting wool, bright pink

¼ skein felting wool, orange

¼ skein felting wool, moss green

10 × 12 in. (25 × 30 cm) bubble wrap
   (hardware store)

1 wooden bead, ø 2 cm, beaded with
   orange seed beads (hobby store)

Rubber mat

Gauze, laundry sprinkler

Bowl with warm water

Curd or olive oil soap

Sewing needle

Felt cutter or carpet knife

TECHNIQUE + TIPS

The bag is made in one piece and takes a long time to create. All the parts are worked in four layers. Make sure that the bubble wrap doesn't slip during the felting process, as it separates the front part of the bag from the back! Make sure you check this regularly by reaching into the bag with your fingers and straightening the bubble wrap. During the 'soaping' stage, the loose ends of the fibres should remain dry. They are used to join the front and back, and if they once get wet they won't mesh together with the other fibres.

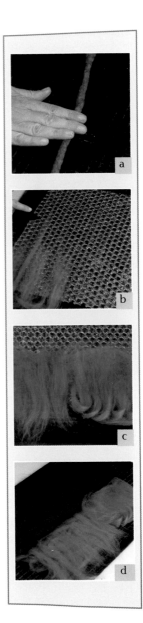

1. Begin with the handle: separate off ⅓ of the bright blue felting wool along its whole length. Take this strand and at each end again divide 6 in. (15 cm) into two separate strands. Leave these open; you're not going to felt them yet.

2. Without wetting, roll the middle part on the mat until the fibres lock together (**illustration a**). Now add a little water and soap, and continue to roll. Make sure that the strand remains an even thickness. Continue to work the strand and wash the soap out once it is firm.

3. Now start on the bag: round off the corners of the bubble wrap, and 7 in. (18 cm) from the bottom of the longer edge cut a small semicircle at both sides (**illustration b**).

4. Lay the first layer of the base colours, bright blue and wine red, on the lower part of the 10 × 12 in. (18 × 25 cm) piece of bubble wrap, one colour on each side. Lay the first layer lengthwise. Leave a ¾ in. (2 cm) overhang at the lower edge (**illustrations b + c**).

5. Now place the second layer in the same colour at right angles to the first, this time leaving a ¾ in. (2 cm) overhang at either side (**illustration d**).

6. Repeat Steps 4 and 5 for the flap, except in this case, the ends of the fibres should not overhang the bubble wrap, but be looped back on themselves exactly on the cut edge of the bubble wrap (**illustration d**).

e

f

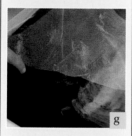

g

h

i

7. Next, lay the pre-cut gauze over the top and sprinkle with water. Dip your fingers in the soap mixture and stroke the wool until the felting process begins. Now you can press harder. Once the material is firm enough, remove the gauze carefully and turn everything over (**illustrations e–g**). The bubble wrap will now be on the top.

8. The next bit is easy. Simply repeat Steps 4, 5 and 6. To give you a firm edge at the top of the front of the bag, make sure when you lay the first layer for the front that you loop the fibres at the top back on themselves, as you did for the flap in Step 6.

9. Again, place the gauze over the top, sprinkle with warm water and stroke the wool with your fingers, remembering to dip them regularly into the soapy water. Once the wool has started to felt you should press more firmly using the palms of the hands (**illustrations i + j**).

10. Now wrap the edges of the bag in the gauze, roll it carefully towards the inside and press it gently together (**illustration k**). This will make the overlapping fibres bond. Make sure the bubble wrap is still positioned correctly.

11. Take the handle and lay the twisted ends next to the notches in the bubble wrap. At each end take one of the opened out 6 in. (15 cm) strands and lay it diagonally across the front of the bag (**illustration l**).

12. For layers 3 and 4 of the bag: lay the plucked out fibres from the other colours in roughly even widths lengthways across the front of the bag. As before, leave the ends at the bottom to overhang by ¾ in. (2 cm), and at the top loop them over so they fit exactly. Next, pluck out short fibres in the same colours – or, if you like, one stripe in a contrasting colour – and lay them across the respective lengthways strips. By doing this you cover and also fix the handle into place on the front (**illustrations m + n**).

13. Lay the gauze over the felt and repeat Step 9.

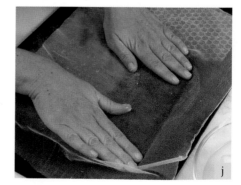

j

k

14. Then carefully remove the gauze and turn the whole lot over again. Now take the other two 6 in. (15 cm) strands from the handle and lay them diagonally over the back of the bag. Then repeat Steps 12 and 13 to complete the back of the bag (**illustration o**).

15. Once the bag has firmed up, carefully roll it up and down several times, keeping the gauze in place. Then do the same thing from right to left. This allows the material to become felted without losing shape. Always roll parallel to the basic shape, never diagonally! Check regularly to see if the gauze is sticking to the wool. Then remove it (**illustration p**).

16. When the bubble wrap puckers, you will know that the bag is shrinking and that it's time for the next step. Wash the soap out under hot water and work the bag firmly. The bubble wrap should still be inside!

17. Finally, pull your bag into shape again and remove the bubble wrap. Then it is best to roll the bag up in a hand towel to dry.

18. Once the bag is completely dry, use the felt cutter to cut a buttonhole in the front. Be very careful and cut little by little until the hole is the right size. The very last step is to sew the wooden ball on as a fastener.

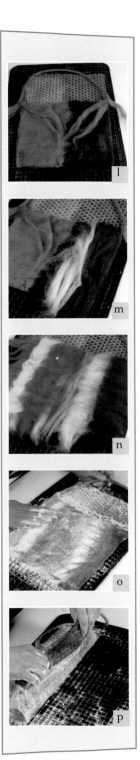

l

m

n

o

p

PART 4

Making your own jewellery...

... Appendix

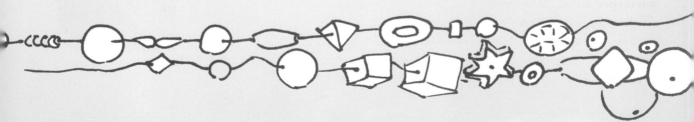

Easy to find... sources

The easiest and most personal way to obtain the materials required is to buy them from specialist retailers of crafting and jewellery-making supplies. You can see the colours, touch the materials, receive personal advice and get new inspiration. However, the Internet also offers numerous possibilities. Here are a few addresses that sell crafting materials online.

www.artbeads.com
A great source of all kinds of supplies, including Swarovski® beads and rhinestones.

www.beadworks.com
Here you'll find beads made from gemstones, precious metals, glass, porcelain, bone, resin, acrylic... the list seems endless.

www.beadstore.com
Specializes in beads and embellishments from places such as Turkey, China, Africa and Asia.

www.rings-things.com
More than 20,000 jewellery-making products plus other jewellery information and a gemstone index.

www.firemountaingems.com
Beads, findings, chains, pearls, displays for your jewellery, stringing material... there's even an online encycloBEADia.™

www.specialistcrafts.co.uk
www.homecrafts.co.uk
Try these two UK-based websites for your Colour Melt Crystals. You can buy online only from Specialist Crafts. You can buy online from HomeCrafts Direct or by phoning HomeCrafts Direct on 0116 269 7733.

Easy to find... jewellery

Bracelets and necklaces

Charm bracelet,
Page 38

Glass bead necklace,
Page 34

Name bracelet with
Swarovski® beads,
Page 50

Antique necklace,
Page 53

"Oriental" bracelet,
Page 72

Blue bead necklace,
Page 68

Turquoise necklace with
satin tie, Page 74

Rings, earrings and hip chains

Flower ring with garnets and Murano glass, Page 42

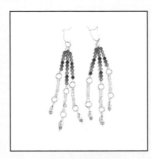

Swarovski® earrings, Page 60

Ring with cultured pearls and garnets, Page 70

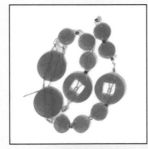

Orange hip chain, Page 62

Glass bead earrings, Page 34

Heart belt, Page 77

Double hoop earrings with mother-of-pearl discs, Page 48

Red hip chain, Page 78

Anklets and accessories

Anklet with hearts,
page 40

Mobile phone beaded dangle,
page 80

'Arabian Nights' anklet,
page 65

Mobile phone bag,
page 82

Crystal ball pendant,
page 44

Jewellery bag,
page 86

Dragonfly hair comb,
page 56

... according to level of difficulty

Picture credits:

All photographs:
Ruprecht Stempell, Cologne, apart from:

Corbis: Hugh Siton/zefa (9),
Summerfield Press (10, 11 top),
Bettman (11 bottom),
Tanguy Loyzance (13), Henry Diltz (14),
AFP/AFP/Getty Images (12),
A. Koblinger/Photocase (7),
waugi/Photocase (8)